O COME EMMANUEL

Reflections on the Advent Antiphons

Jane Williams • Chris Russell • Esther Prior • Philip North
Muthuraj Swamy • Tanya Marlow • David Hoyle • Lucy Winkett

CHURCH HOUSE
PUBLISHING

Contents

About the contributors

ABOUT THE AUTHORS

Jane Williams is McDonald Professor in Christian Theology at St Mellitus College.

Chris Russell is Vicar of St Dionis Parsons Green and a former Advisor for Evangelism and Witness to the Archbishop of Canterbury.

Esther Prior is the Bishop of Aston.

Philip North is the Bishop of Blackburn.

Muthuraj Swamy is the Director of the Cambridge Centre for Christianity Worldwide.

Tanya Marlow is an author, speaker and broadcaster on faith and spirituality.

David Hoyle is the Dean of Westminster.

Lucy Winkett is Rector of St James's Piccadilly and Priest-in-Charge of St Pancras Euston Road.

ABOUT THE ARTIST

SunYoung Kim is a Korean illustrator and visual storyteller. At Yeyesisters, she creates faith-based art that reflects God's love, hope, and the beauty of nature.

Introduction:
The Advent O Antiphons

The Advent O Antiphons have been part of the Church's liturgical tradition at least since the early Middle Ages. Their roots go back to sixth- or seventh-century practice. These antiphons or refrains all begin with 'O …' and were sung at Vespers (Evening Prayer) on the seven days preceding Christmas Eve (17–23 December).

The Antiphons are addressed to God, calling for him to come as teacher and deliverer. They contain a tapestry of scriptural titles and pictures that describe God's saving work in Christ. Each antiphon calls on Jesus using a *title* – Wisdom, Key of David, Morning Star, and so on. Each title reveals something of Jesus' divine identity and saving mission.

The title is followed each time by an *attribute* or *act* associated with that title. Each antiphon concludes with a heartfelt plea: *Veni!* 'Come!' Together the antiphons form a profound theological meditation on the coming of the Messiah.

Each of the titles at the start of the antiphons is drawn from the Old Testament prophets. Each one speaks to a different aspect of Christ's identity. Taken together, they create a rich mosaic of expectation and promise. When read in reverse, the first letters of each title (Sapientia, Adonai, Radix, Clavis, Oriens, Rex, Emmanuel) form an acrostic – *ERO CRAS*. This is Latin for 'I will be [with you] tomorrow'. This hidden message adds a final touch of rhetorical elegance, reinforcing the immediacy of Christ's coming.

It is not known when the antiphons were composed, or by whom, but they were already in use by the eighth century. These antiphons have inspired one of the most beloved Advent hymns, 'O Come, O Come, Emmanuel'. Each verse is a poetic rendering of an O Antiphon, translated and versified in the nineteenth century from earlier Latin texts. Through this hymn, the rich imagery and theological hope of the antiphons reach the hearts of congregations year after year.

In the medieval rite of Salisbury Cathedral, in common use in England before the Reformation, the antiphons began on 16 December. There was also an additional antiphon ('O Virgin of virgins') on 23 December. This tradition is reflected in the Calendar of the Book of Common Prayer, where 16 December is designated O Sapientia (O Wisdom). The *Common Worship* Calendar has adopted the more widely used form.

The O Antiphons do not stand alone. Most obviously, they frame the Magnificat, Mary's great song of praise, sung daily at Evening Prayer. Their resonance with the message of the Magnificat is not incidental. The Magnificat proclaims the reversal of worldly expectations – the mighty are cast down, the lowly lifted up, the hungry are filled with good things. The antiphons, meanwhile, proclaim the coming of the one who will bring this about: the Wisdom of God, the Root of Jesse, the Key of David.

The two texts are in dynamic conversation. Mary's song shows the interior posture of faith – humble, expectant, rejoicing in God's promises; the antiphons show the one who fulfils them. Thus, the pairing of the Magnificat with each of these cries – *Veni!* – enfolds the Advent longing into the story of salvation. Together, they help us to enter into a rhythm of prayer, in which the Church, like Mary, becomes the dwelling place of the Word through hope, praise and obedience.

In *Common Worship: Daily Prayer*, the use of antiphons or refrains is not limited to those at the Magnificat in the final days of Advent. The Church's liturgy throughout the year uses antiphons. They are used to frame the canticles of Morning and Evening Prayer – the Benedictus and Magnificat. These antiphons often highlight the observance or season. They link the daily rhythm of prayer to the wider celebration of salvation history. In every case, they draw attention to the significance of the canticle itself. This is just as the O Antiphons bring out the richness of the Magnificat in Advent.

The O Antiphons are not isolated curiosities of the Advent season; they are part of a wider and deeper liturgical tradition. They invite us to pray with longing, to recognize Christ in his many scriptural titles. They tell to allow the Magnificat – Mary's song, and the Church's song – to be expanded by the cry, *Come, Lord Jesus!*

How to use this book

This booklet is designed to help you deepen your connection with God during the Advent season. It contains twenty-four reflections centred around the 'O Antiphons' – the ancient texts on which the hymn 'O Come, O Come, Emmanuel' is based.

Each day contains a Bible reading, a reflection, an invitation to respond and a short prayer. There are also eight paintings commissioned for this volume from artist SunYoung Kim (see pages 13–15 for her introduction to these images).

You can use this booklet:

ON YOUR OWN:

- Set aside five minutes each day to follow a reflection from the booklet – whether it's first thing in the morning, at lunchtime or before bed.
- You might like to keep an Advent journal. Writing down your responses, questions and passages that resonated with you can be a powerful way to keep track of your journey through Advent.
- During Advent 2025, you could also listen to the reflections on the Everyday Faith app from the Church of England. Find out more and download via **cofe.io/EverydayFaithApp**

IN A GROUP:

- Encourage your group to meet regularly to discuss the preceding three to six days. Share how the reflections are shaping your understanding of Advent. Pray for the challenges that arose to you this week.

- Have one person each day to share a brief insight or personal application from the day's devotional; encourage members to share prayer requests related to the day's theme.

- You might want to use or adapt some of the ideas about music and worship below to shape a time of quiet reflection and prayer at the end of the session.

GOING FURTHER

There are a variety of creative ways to explore the antiphons during Advent both at church and at home. Various ways to do this – many of them drawn or adapted from *Together for a Season Volume 1* (Church House Publishing, 2006) – are suggested below.

Further suggestions, resources and links can be found on the Church of England website via **www.cofe.io/OComeEmmanuel**

USING THE ADVENT ANTIPHONS IN WORSHIP

Traditionally, the Advent antiphons are used with the Magnificat from 17–23 December. If you pray Evening Prayer daily, this is the ideal setting. But they can also enrich other forms of prayer – at home, in church or in groups – reminding us that the baby in the manger is also the long-awaited Messiah.

MUSICAL SETTINGS OF THE ADVENT ANTIPHONS

From their earliest days, the Advent antiphons have been sung alongside the Magnificat at Evening Prayer in the days leading up to Christmas Eve. Many churches and cathedrals continue this ancient tradition: one of these is Westminster Abbey. The Abbey's website features an informative page exploring the Advent antiphons, with links to free video performances of the traditional plainsong settings in both Latin and English: **www.westminster-abbey.org/the-great-o-antiphons**

The Church of England has also commissioned new choral settings of the *Common Worship* translation of the antiphons (as used in this book) from a range of contemporary composers including Philip Moore, Bernadette Farrell and Thomas Hewitt-Jones. Free video versions (sung by St Martin's Voices) will be available via **cofe.io/OComeEmmanuel**

Finally, the Church of England's *Daily Prayer* app features the antiphons in its audio Evening Prayer services from 17 December: **cofe.io/DailyPrayer**

FINDING OR CREATING THE SYMBOLS

In addition to SunYoung Kim's paintings of the 'O Antiphons' included in this volume, there are numerous other artistic representations of them online, including a set of banners created by The Benedictine Sisters of Turvey Abbey.

There are also simple symbols that can be downloaded and used as templates for making your own symbols (downloadable via **www.cofe.io/OComeEmmanuel**).

- Use gold card or coloured paper to cut out simple shapes.
- Create wire or ribbon circles (for the 'O') with a symbol inside.
- Try clay, embroidery, or even stained-glass-style tissue paper.
- Adapt ideas from Advent decorations – such as wooden stars on sticks – to reflect each antiphon.

USING THE ANTIPHONS AT HOME

You could use the antiphons as daily prayers – at meals or bedtime. Light a candle for each day, perhaps using coloured candles or decorated jars.

You might source symbols or pictures online for the antiphons or design your own. You could decorate your Christmas tree gradually, adding one antiphon symbol each day from 17 December.

If your household enjoys singing, include verses of 'O Come, O Come, Emmanuel' – even young children should quickly learn and be able to join in with the refrain. You might also use the simple prayers suggested below.

SIMPLE PRAYERS FOR EACH ANTIPHON

As well as the prayers suggested at the end of each reflection in *O Come, Emmanuel*, these short, simple prayers could be used at home or in small groups, especially from 17–23 December:

Come, O Adonai, who appeared to Moses in the burning bush,
and gave him the Law on Mount Sinai;
Come, Adonai, and save us. Amen.

Come, O Root of Jesse, be a sign among the peoples;
Come, Root of Jesse, and deliver us now. Amen.

Come, O Key of David, free the captives and those in darkness;
Come, Key of David, lead us into light. Amen.

Come, O Morning Star, Everlasting Light;
Come, Morning Star, and shine on us. Amen.

Come, O King of the Nations, save us your creatures;
Come, King of the Nations, save us now. Amen.

Come, O Emmanuel, God with us;
Come, Emmanuel, and save us. Amen.

USING THE ANTIPHONS IN CHURCH

You might dedicate a space in your church to Advent books, images and prayer cards to encourage others to take part. Make it a welcoming space for anyone to pause and reflect.

At the end of Evening Prayer, those attending might move to a symbolic location (or 'station') in your church that reflects the antiphon's theme. For example:

- **17 December – Wisdom**: the altar/holy table
- **18 December – Adonai**: the lectern/reading desk
- **19 December – Root of Jesse**: the Christmas tree
- **20 December – Key of David**: the church door
- **21 December – Morning Star**: outside, to look at the stars or sun
- **22 December – King of the Nations**: a foundation stone or arch
- **23 December – Emmanuel**: the crib.

At each station, you might light a candle, say (or listen to a sung version of) the antiphon together, and perhaps add a short prayer (like those suggested above).

About the paintings

These eight illustrations were created using traditional Korean watercolour on delicate rice paper, chosen to evoke a sense of gentleness and refinement while offering a fresh visual expression of familiar Advent symbols.

Inspired by the beauty of God's creation – flowers, trees, animals, mountains and seas – the natural world becomes a central language for expressing the longing and hope reflected in the Advent Antiphons and the Magnificat (The Song of Mary). Each image is rich with biblical symbolism, thoughtfully woven to invite prayerful reflection.

The colour palette centres on soft, natural tones: blue to evoke life and depth; gentle greens for growth and peace; and warm touches of gold and pink, suggesting divine royalty and tenderness.

By reimagining the Advent story through a traditional medium, these works draw together the promises of the Old Testament and the fulfilment of them Christians find in the New. Across time, they point to the same unchanging truth: the coming of Jesus Christ, our Saviour and King. They invite us into wonder, peace and joyful expectation.

O WISDOM

A book, the word of God, opens in the sky, releasing a river of life of Jesus that brings order and flourishing to creation. Echoing the Korean tradition of *Irworobongdo* – a stylized landscape painting associated with royalty – this image honours Jesus Christ as the eternal Wisdom and true King, shaping the cosmos with love and truth.

O ADONAI

Amid darkness, a fiery bush glows alive but unconsumed as Moses encounters God's holy presence. In this depiction, its branches form outstretched arms, pointing to Christ on the cross. This holy fire is both a calling and promise: the God who once saved by power now saves through love.

O ROOT OF JESSE

From a cut stump grows a flourishing tree with fruits, implying life emerging from what seemed dead. The root represents the lineage of David into which Jesus was born. Through him, people can have new life and spiritual abundance. A wolf and a lamb represent the kingdom of the Messiah (echoing the peaceable kingdom envisioned in Isaiah 11).

O KEY OF DAVID

A dove, the Holy Spirit, bears a golden key, flying toward the dawn. Behind it, light begins to break through the night's shadow, hinting at God's plan for redemption. Jesus Christ, the Key of David, opens what no one can shut, unlocking hearts and freeing the world from fear and darkness.

O MORNING STAR

Like the image for O Wisdom, the landscape depicted here draws on the conventions used in the Korean tradition of *Irworobongdo*. A single radiant star lights the deep indigo sky.

Below, the world waits in shadow. As dawn breaks, the true King rises in glory. Jesus, the Morning Star, heralds hope, healing and the coming of God's eternal kingdom.

O KING OF THE NATIONS

A moon jar (similar in shape to the globe) made from earth has been broken but is now mended with golden fissures. It becomes a vessel of beauty and restoration. The golden crown represents Christ, the true King, who heals what is broken and draws all nations into unity.

O EMMANUEL

Under blooming trees, a newborn baby lies in a manger. Around him hang emblems of kingship, justice, light and divine authority. God with us arrives not in splendour, but in stillness and peace, turning the world upside down through humble love and sacrifice.

MAGNIFICAT

Mary and her cousin Elizabeth meet in joyful embrace. There is movement, blessing and boldness here, the prophetic spirit of Mary's song. A golden cross points to Christ's redemptive purpose and the path of love that will pierce Mary's own soul.

SUNYOUNG KIM
LONDON, MAY 2025

O Sapientia

O Wisdom, coming forth from the mouth
of the Most High,
reaching from one end to the other mightily,
and sweetly ordering all things:
Come and teach us the way of prudence.

cf. Ecclesiasticus 24.3; Wisdom 8.1

O come, thou Wisdom from on high!
Who madest all in earth and sky,
Creating man from dust and clay:
To us reveal salvation's way.

Rejoice! Rejoice! Emmanuel
Shall come to thee, O Israel.

Latin hymn based on the Advent Antiphons, Cologne 1710
English translation by T. A. Lacey (1853–1931) and others

O Wisdom

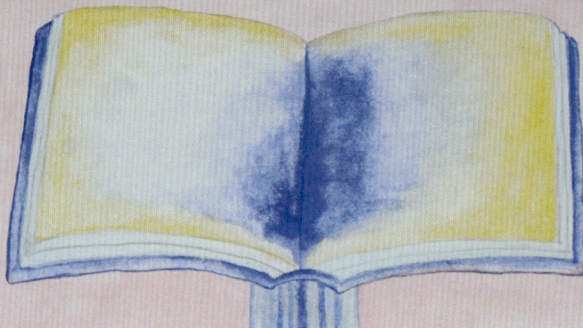

Day One
WISDOM ALIVE

READING Proverbs 2.1-11

For the Lord gives wisdom;
  from his mouth come knowledge and understanding
he stores up sound wisdom for the upright;
  he is a shield to those who walk blamelessly,
guarding the paths of justice
  and preserving the way of his faithful ones.
Then you will understand righteousness and justice
  and equity, every good path;
for wisdom will come into your heart,
  and knowledge will be pleasant to your soul;

REFLECTION

Wisdom is a lifetime's search. It is something longed for but not acquired easily. It is a gift from God, rather than innate to human beings. As such, we have to yearn for it, because God does not force gifts upon us.

The seekers in this passage in Proverbs have to use all their skills. They have to work out when to listen and when to shout, when to search and when to wait. When they gain wisdom, it will not be just for their own pleasure. Instead, they will see into the character of God's own wisdom.

Human wisdom is learning to care about justice and equity and faithfulness. These are qualities that, by definition, cannot be exercised in solitude. They commit us to a way of interacting with others. They commit us to at least starting to love the world as God does.

When the seekers start out to search for the treasure of wisdom, it seems like an abstract quality. But gradually, Wisdom comes alive, and keeps them company on the journey, as friend and guardian. The closer the seekers come to the Lord, the more apparent it becomes that to walk in wisdom is to walk with God's own presence.

JANE WILLIAMS

RESPONSE

Wisdom is a gift from God, but it must be used for others. How might seeing it like that help us to seek for it?

PRAYER

Jesus, living Wisdom,
teach us your ways of gentleness and peace.
Walk them with us and all your faithful people,
until we come together to your kingdom,
where justice and mercy, holiness and love
come hand in hand to greet us.
Amen.

Day Two
WISDOM IN TOUGH TIMES

READING Psalm 90

When you are angry, all our days are gone;
our years come to an end like a sigh …

So teach us to number our days
that we may apply our hearts to wisdom.

REFLECTION

Psalm 90 contrasts God's eternal life with the brevity and insignificance of human life. The psalmist is finding it hard to believe that God even notices us, let alone cares about us. How many people must God have seen come and go since he first brought the world into existence? But the psalmist is not just feeling like insignificant dust in God's sight. It is not just God's indifference that is weighing upon the writer, but what feels like God's active anger.

The turning point of the Psalm comes in verse 12. The psalmist realizes it is possible to live even a brief life with wisdom. And suddenly, as that thought breaks through, God no longer seems distant, careless, threatening, but full of faithful love.

God's love is able to give lasting meaning and joy to everything we do, even in our ephemeral lives. We cannot do that for ourselves, but we can rely on God. The eternal God is not indifferent towards us. And so, even in tough times – when we cannot see any point in our own lives – we can hope and trust in the faithfulness of God, who brought all things into being out of love.

JANE WILLIAMS

RESPONSE

Where in your life are you in danger of falling into despair?
Pray for a wise heart that leads to trust in the weeks and months to come.

PRAYER

Almighty God,
our eternal refuge,
teach us to live with the knowledge of our death
and to rejoice in the promise of your glory,
revealed to us in Jesus Christ our Lord.
Amen.

Day Three
THE SPIRIT OF WISDOM

READING 1 Corinthians 2.1-11

I came to you in weakness and in fear and in much trembling. My speech and my proclamation were not with plausible words of wisdom, but with a demonstration of the Spirit and of power, so that your faith might rest not on human wisdom but on the power of God.

… these things God has revealed to us through the Spirit; for the Spirit searches everything, even the depths of God.

REFLECTION

The Christians in Corinth in today's reading come across as rather pleased with themselves. They are sure of their understanding of the Gospel and excited by the exercise of the showy gifts of the Spirit.

In response, Paul is trying to help them see beyond themselves to the reality of God. Paul points out that he wasn't on top form when preaching in Corinth. Even so, somehow, the Holy Spirit was able to use Paul and fill him with a power not his own. Now Paul wants the Corinthian Christians to realize that that's the power we all need to rely on: the power of the mysterious, secret wisdom of God.

There are no pathways of our own devising to get to that wisdom, however brilliant we may think we are. We only know God because God invites us into understanding. There is no abstract knowledge of God, only God's self-gift in the Holy Spirit.

In their arrogant assessment of their own wisdom, the people in power at the time crucified Jesus. That is a warning to the Corinthians and to us. We need to learn from the Spirit of wisdom before we can exercise wisdom.

JANE WILLIAMS

RESPONSE

What is the difference between *having* knowledge and *living with* wisdom? How does wisdom shape who we are?

PRAYER

O Wisdom, coming forth from the mouth of the Most High,
reaching from one end to the other,
mightily and sweetly ordering all things:
Come and teach us the way of prudence.
Amen.

O Adonai

(18 DECEMBER)

O Adonai, and leader of the House of Israel,
who appeared to Moses in the fire
of the burning bush
and gave him the law on Sinai:
Come and redeem us
with an outstretched arm.

cf. Exodus 3.2; 24.12

O come, O come, Adonai,
Who in thy glorious majesty
From Sinai's mountain, clothed with awe,
Gavest thy folk the ancient law.

Rejoice! Rejoice! Emmanuel
Shall come to thee, O Israel.

O Adonai

Day Four
CLOSE

READING Exodus 3.1-6

God called to him out of the bush, 'Moses, Moses!' And he said, 'Here I am.' Then he said, 'Come no closer! Remove the sandals from your feet, for the place on which you are standing is holy ground.' He said further, 'I am the God of your father, the God of Abraham, the God of Isaac, and the God of Jacob.' And Moses hid his face, for he was afraid to look at God.

REFLECTION

I always loved playing hide-and-seek – the moments when you have hidden and hear the seeker coming to find you – even holding your breath not to give yourself away.

Scripture is one long story of hide-and-seek – we're the habitual hiders; God is the relentless, eternal seeker.

Moses is hiding. It's not the first time. Right after he was born, his mother hid him in a basket. But now he is hiding because his anger was so fiery and consuming he'd killed an Egyptian. He has disappeared into the wilderness to save himself. The distance is physical, emotional and spiritual.

But here the Lord – Adonai – comes close. We notice how God comes close.

The bush burns but isn't consumed. Unlike Moses and his fury. He is called. Double named even, 'Moses, Moses'. Only seven people in Scripture get that.

Will he stop? Will he come out from hiding? Will he come near? Yes. He turns aside, comes close – 'Here I am'. Close to the great Lord who has come to seek him out. The Lord makes up all the distance. Ironically, we're told Moses hid his face – afraid to look at the Lord.

God's closeness is not easily borne.

CHRIS RUSSELL

RESPONSE

How might God be getting your attention – coming close to you – in these days of Advent? Will you turn aside – or come close?

PRAYER

Lord God,
sustain us in this vale of tears
with the vision of your grace and glory,
that, strengthened by the bread of life,
we may come to your eternal dwelling place;
in the power of Jesus Christ our Lord.
Amen.

Day Five
FREE HANDS

READING Exodus 6.1-8

'Say therefore to the Israelites, "I am the Lord, and I will free you from the burdens of the Egyptians and deliver you from slavery to them. I will redeem you with an outstretched arm and with mighty acts of judgement."'

REFLECTION

Our hands are remarkable. Each is composed of 27 bones, 29 joints, at least 123 ligaments, 34 muscles, 48 nerves and 30 arteries; 56 of the 206 bones in your body are in your hands.

We rarely have empty hands – they're holding things, carrying things, working at things, giving and taking things. The Hebrew slaves didn't have free hands – they had no choice but to put their hands to demanding manual labour. Imagine the toll on their hands: bound and restricted, controlled and constrained, burdened and powerless. Hands enslaved.

Yet Exodus tells us the Lord is compelled to reach out his arm and bring an end to this slavery. The image of the 'outstretched arm' is everywhere in Scripture. It is deliberate, active and consequential.

The Lord acts freely to liberate the hands of his people in slavery. Their Exodus to freedom is entirely his doing. This is the kind of Lord he is.

When the Lord Jesus comes among us, stretching out his actual arm to free us, we of course aren't having any of it. We put nails through his hands. But it is his free choice to give himself for us that sets us our hands free.

CHRIS RUSSELL

RESPONSE

Consider your hands. What are you carrying? What feels beyond your grasp? What does the Lord's outstretched arm free these hands for?

PRAYER

Lord God, we stretch our hands to you.
Help us to let go of our burdens,
and give grace that we may worthily carry
the gifts that your Son has purchased for us with his blood.
Amen.

Day Six
OTHER

READING Exodus 24.12-18

Then Moses went up on the mountain, and the cloud covered the mountain. The glory of the Lord settled on Mount Sinai, and the cloud covered it for six days; on the seventh day he called to Moses out of the cloud. Now the appearance of the glory of the Lord was like a devouring fire on the top of the mountain in the sight of the people of Israel.

REFLECTION

A rabbi once told me that the key to all relationships was differentiation. Having a sense of your own edges and boundaries. It's not about standing your ground, but being the gift of a distinct other person to them.

Our reading today is full of Hollywood movie effects: a mountain with fire and cloud. The conditions are not pleasant. The visuals are not easy on the eye. The terrain is dangerous and the requirements demanding.

But this is Adonai – the Lord – we are talking about.

Today we are invited into an uneasy place where we recognize the Lord as Other. Not as some extension of our best ways, our profoundest hopes or most beautiful vistas. But as the Lord who asks us (in the words of Psalm 50): 'Did you think that I am even such a one as yourself?' The Lord who is distinct from us in his loving, knowing, creating and redeeming. The Lord who is free.

And in that freedom he chooses to draw near to us. Not to consume us or absorb us, but so that we might realize who we truly are: created beings, distinct, unique and called.

CHRIS RUSSELL

RESPONSE

Spend some moments contemplating how different God is. Feel the weight of it. Glimpse the glory.

PRAYER

Mighty God,
dwelling in unapproachable light,
forgive our vain attempts to appease you,
and show us your full salvation
in Jesus Christ your Son our Lord.
Amen.

O Radix Jesse

O Root of Jesse, standing as a sign
among the peoples;
before you kings will shut their mouths,
to you the nations will make their prayer:
Come and deliver us, and delay no longer.

cf. Isaiah 11.10; 45.14; 52.15; Romans 15.12

O come, thou Root of Jesse! Draw
The quarry from the lion's claw;
From those dread caverns of the grave,
From nether hell, thy people save.

Rejoice! Rejoice! Emmanuel
Shall come to thee, O Israel.

O Root of Jesse

Day Seven
A SIGN AMONG THE PEOPLES

READING Isaiah 11.1-9

A shoot shall come out from the stock of Jesse,
*   and a branch shall grow out of his roots.*

The spirit of the Lord shall rest on him,
*   the spirit of wisdom and understanding,*
*   the spirit of counsel and might,*
*   the spirit of knowledge and the fear of the Lord.*

REFLECTION

In a world marked by turmoil and uncertainty, the promise of the Root of Jesse stands firm. Today's reading offers a vision of hope: 'A shoot will come up from the stump of Jesse; from his roots a Branch will bear fruit.' This is no ordinary descendant. Jesus is the fulfilment of that promise, both the Branch and the Root. He is the One on whom the Spirit of the Lord rests. In him we find wisdom, understanding, counsel and strength.

When everything around us feels unstable, he remains the unshakable sign among the nations, the One through whom God's redemptive plan is unfolding. He does not judge by appearances or decide by hearsay. With righteousness he judges the needy. With justice he gives decisions for the poor.

The world seeks fleeting security in power, wealth and influence, but Isaiah's vision reminds us that true peace comes through Christ alone. His presence confronts injustice and brings hope where there is despair.

This Advent, as we wait and prepare, let us lift our eyes to Jesus, our unfailing sign of God's faithfulness, our Root of Jesse. He is the One who reigns in truth and promises a kingdom where all shall dwell in peace.

ESTHER PRIOR

RESPONSE

Where do you place your hope when life feels uncertain?

PRAYER

Lord Jesus, Root of Jesse,
help me to stand firm in you,
trusting that your justice and righteousness will prevail.
May I be a sign of your hope
in a world that desperately needs you.
Amen.

Day Eight
KINGS WILL SHUT THEIR MOUTHS

READING Romans 15.7-13

'The root of Jesse shall come,
    the one who rises to rule the Gentiles;
in him the Gentiles shall hope.'

May the God of hope fill you with all joy and peace in believing, so that you may abound in hope by the power of the Holy Spirit.

REFLECTION

The rulers of this world wield power as if it will last forever. But Scripture tells us of a day when they will fall silent before the true King. As Isaiah foretold: 'The Root of Jesse will spring up, one who will arise to rule over the nations; in him the Gentiles will hope.' Paul echoes Isaiah's words in today's reading. This is the Christ we wait for in Advent, the One before whom even kings will shut their mouths in awe (Isaiah 52.15). Earthly power is temporary; God's reign is eternal.

When Jesus returns, those who have boasted in their strength will be left speechless. The nations will turn to him with hope and worship. Paul writes that this promise is for all people. The Gentiles too 'may glorify God for his mercy'.

Injustice may seem to flourish now, but its days are numbered. Christ is coming, and his rule will bring perfect justice and peace. As we wait, let us not grow weary but instead hold fast to the One who holds all authority. Let us live in hope, joy and peace, abounding in the power of the Holy Spirit as we trust that His kingdom is near.

ESTHER PRIOR

RESPONSE

How does the promise of Christ's ultimate authority change the way you respond to injustice today?

PRAYER

King Jesus,
silence the arrogance of this world
and turn our hearts toward you.
Help me to trust in your power and pray with expectation
for the day when all will acknowledge your rule.
Amen.

Day Nine
DELIVER US

READING Isaiah 42.1-9

Here is my servant, whom I uphold,
my chosen, in whom my soul delights;
I have put my spirit upon him;
he will bring forth justice to the nations.
He will not cry or lift up his voice,
or make it heard in the street;
a bruised reed he will not break,
and a dimly burning wick he will not quench;
he will faithfully bring forth justice.
He will not grow faint or be crushed
until he has established justice in the earth;
and the coastlands wait for his teaching.

REFLECTION

Maranatha! Come, Lord Jesus!

Advent is a season of longing, a time to cry out for the fulfilment of God's promises. In today's reading, we are given a vision of the

Servant of the Lord, who will bring justice to the nations. This Servant, Jesus Christ, does not shout or break the bruised reed. Instead, he faithfully establishes justice with quiet strength and unwavering purpose.

We see suffering, brokenness and injustice all around us. We long for Christ to return and set things right. But our longing is not passive. It shapes how we live now. When we desire his coming, we learn to seek his kingdom first, to walk humbly and act justly, to be bearers of light in the darkness.

The Root of Jesse has come, fulfilling the promises of old, and he will come again. Until that day, we wait, not in despair, but in expectation. We know that the one who began a good work will bring it to completion. As Isaiah declares, new things are springing forth – do we not perceive them?

This Advent, may our hearts burn with longing. May our lives reflect the deep, living hope that he is near and will not delay forever.

ESTHER PRIOR

RESPONSE

How does the hope of Christ's return shape the way you live today?

PRAYER

Lord Jesus,
stir in me a deep longing for your coming.
May my heart be ready, my hands be open,
and my life reflect your kingdom as I wait in joyful hope.
Amen.

O Clavis David

(20 DECEMBER)

O Key of David and sceptre of the House of Israel;
you open and no one can shut;
you shut and no one can open:
Come and lead the prisoners from the prison house,
those who dwell in darkness and the shadow of death.

cf. Isaiah 22.22; 42.7

O come, thou Lord of David's Key!
The royal door fling wide and free;
Safeguard for us the heavenward road,
And bar the way to death's abode.

Rejoice! Rejoice! Emmanuel
Shall come to thee, O Israel.

Latin hymn based on the Advent Antiphons, Cologne 1710
English translation by T. A. Lacey (1853–1931) and others

O Key of David

Day Ten
KEY TO FREEDOM

READING Isaiah 22.20-23

I will commit your authority to his hand, and he shall be a father to the inhabitants of Jerusalem and to the house of Judah. I will place on his shoulder the key of the house of David; he shall open, and no one shall shut; he shall shut, and no one shall open.

REFLECTION

When the Syrian rebels toppled the Assad regime in December 2024, the first place they headed for was the prisons. They got the key and headed to the unspeakable underground dungeons, the hallmark of tyranny. They flung open the doors and released prisoners into the light of day. Some of them had been incarcerated their whole life.

We may live in a democracy and value our freedom, but in reality, we too are prisoners. We are captive to sin, captive to our failing bodies, captive to death. We need a rescuer.

And that rescuer is Jesus who is the key. Through his birth in Bethlehem, he enters our prison cell and makes himself a victim to human sin. Through the cross, he throws open the cell doors of our captivity and sets us free. He leads us out blinking into the dazzling light of eternity.

As we pray 'O Key of David', we embrace the gift of freedom that Christ's coming brings. For that freedom is the source of our joy and the content of our proclamation. As those set free by Christ, we declare freedom to the world.

PHILIP NORTH

RESPONSE

You are free in Christ. Stop for a moment and reflect on what that freedom means for the way you think, act and decide.

PRAYER

Lord Jesus,
You are the Key of David
who liberates us from the darkness of the prison cell
and releases us into the dazzling light of eternal day.
May we never take for granted your gift of freedom,
but rejoice to share it with a captive humanity.
Amen.

Day Eleven
THE DOOR IS OPEN

READING Revelation 3.7-8, 10-13

'And to the angel of the church in Philadelphia write:

These are the words of the holy one, the true one,
who has the key of David,
who opens and no one will shut,
who shuts and no one opens:

Look, I have set before you an open door, which no one is able to shut.'

REFLECTION

I would be a useless prisoner. The thought of the cell door being slammed at night leaving me locked in a tiny room without the key fills me with dread.

But Jesus sets before us an open door. No one can shut it again because Jesus is both the key and key holder. No matter where our lives may go, no matter what sickness, suffering or imprisonment we may have to endure, we have a freedom in Christ. It is a freedom that, by definition, no power in all this world can take away from us.

But in the Lord's prophecy to the church in Philadelphia, this freedom is not simply a source of reassurance. Just as important, it is the springboard for the mission. This tiny church has a freedom in Christ that cannot be taken away. With freedom, they can take risks, declare the gospel and live differently. They needn't fear abuse or persecution because the door that leads to the New Jerusalem is thrown open and cannot be shut.

You are free in Christ. That means you can be bold in your Christian living and take big risks for your faith. Nothing can go wrong, because Christ's liberating work is done.

PHILIP NORTH

RESPONSE

Knowing that you are already free, where and how can you take greater risks for the gospel today?

PRAYER

Lord Jesus,
because of your cross, the door is open and no one can shut it.
Secure in this certain hope,
help us to brave dangers, endure persecution
and risk everything for the gospel,
because we know we are safe in your love for ever.
Amen.

Day Twelve
FREEDOM FIGHTERS

READING Psalm 89.19-29

'I have set a youth above the mighty;
I have raised a young man over the people.

'I have found David my servant;
with my holy oil have I anointed him.

'My hand shall hold him fast
and my arm shall strengthen him.'

REFLECTION

Our God is a God of liberation. In his saving work, he raises up the lowly and the disempowered and gives them freedom.

As Psalm 89 reminds us, this is what God does in his servant David. The lowly shepherd of Bethlehem, overlooked even by his father, is anointed king by the prophet Samuel. Through God's power and protection, he crushes all his foes.

But David's life points us to an even greater work of liberation. In Jesus, born of David's House and line, God himself comes to be our King. The lowly child of Bethlehem, born in poverty, is anointed by the Spirit of God. Through the cross, he reveals himself to be the Saviour King who crushes even sin and death.

As we are liberated by this saving work, we are called to liberate others. We give voice to the refugee and fight for justice for the oppressed. We feed the hungry and prioritize the marginalized. Through these actions, we bear witness to the saving work of God who leads the prisoner from the prison house.

God has raised us up and set us free. So let's hear his call and fight for freedom in his name.

PHILIP NORTH

RESPONSE

Think of the prisoners you will meet today: those who are captive to poverty, injustice, grief or sin. How can you fight for their freedom?

PRAYER

Lord Jesus,
in your saving work you have won the fight for our freedom,
and have sent us to declare freedom to the world.
Give us compassion in service,
courage in striving for justice,
and a sincere love for the poor,
that your liberating power may be made known to all.
Amen.

O Oriens

O Morning Star,
splendour of light eternal and sun of righteousness:
Come and enlighten those who dwell in darkness
and the shadow of death.

cf. Malachi 4.2

O come, O come, thou Dayspring bright!
Pour on our souls thy healing light;
Dispel the long night's lingering gloom,
And pierce the shadows of the tomb.

Rejoice! Rejoice! Emmanuel
Shall come to thee, O Israel.

O Morning Star

Day Thirteen
NO FEAR,
NOT AFRAID

READING Psalm 27.1-8

The Lord is my light and my salvation;
whom then shall I fear?
The Lord is the strength of my life;
of whom then shall I be afraid?

Though a host encamp against me,
my heart shall not be afraid,
and though there rise up war against me,
yet will I put my trust in him.

REFLECTION

'The Lord is my light and salvation,' the psalmist affirms. 'Whom then shall I fear?' What we see here is a statement of faith. A statement of confidence. A statement of complete trust.

The psalmist begins with the image of light. God is light. What is the connection between light and being saved? The connection between light and strength? Between light and having no fear? From our everyday experiences, we know that light gives us clarity. There is no deceit in it. It removes our fear arising from darkness. We can see and be seen. It gives us confidence, leading to trust. We can put our steps forward confidently.

In Jesus' time, many people lived in darkness. The darkness of the Roman occupation. The darkness of oppressive structures in their faith traditions and in society. The darkness of their sins that kept them from God and from each other. People were filled with fear. But God the light came to this world through Jesus. He offered people hope and led them to faith and trust in God, which they needed to overcome darkness and fear. Jesus is the morning star in whom we can confidently trust.

MUTHURAJ SWAMY

RESPONSE

Remember a moment when physical light appeared against extreme darkness. Did you feel strengthened? In what ways does trusting God as light help in your life?

PRAYER

Our sovereign Lord,
Of old you spoke by the mouth of your prophets,
but in our days you speak through your Son,
whom you have appointed the heir of all things.
Grant us, your people, to walk in his light,
for you are our light and our salvation.
Amen.

Day Fourteen
BE HEALED, BE FREE

READING Malachi 4.1-2

See, the day is coming, burning like an oven, when all the arrogant and all evildoers will be stubble; the day that comes shall burn them up, says the Lord of hosts, so that it will leave them neither root nor branch. But for you who revere my name the sun of righteousness shall rise, with healing in its wings. You shall go out leaping like calves from the stall.

REFLECTION

The prophet Malachi prophesied among people in Jerusalem about four centuries before Jesus was born. He invited them to turn from their evil ways and live according to God's commandments. He preached about God's comfort, as the people had been suffering for centuries having been exiled and oppressed by foreign powers.

In chapter 4, Malachi talks about how new light is going to change people's lives. He talks about it in two ways. First, as the destroying and purifying power of fire that burns up all evil. Then, as the rising of the sun of righteousness for those seeking for God. The light from this sun is warm and soothing. It is not a hot fire. There is justice in it, coupled with compassion for those suffering. This light heals them. People go out leaping like calves from the stall. They are free to move around.

Here in the UK, in our daily lives, as spring and summer bring more and more light, our lives change. People are more relaxed. There are more gatherings, more celebrations. In our life as a whole, Jesus is the morning star giving us light – light that is warm, light that heals, light that makes us free and helps us grow.

MUTHURAJ SWAMY

RESPONSE

Reflect on the connection between light, and healing and wellbeing. How does God as light heal our spiritual and social lives, and nurture us to grow?

PRAYER

That the light of God's coming may dawn
on all who live in darkness and the shadow of death;
that God may bind up the broken-hearted,
restore the sick
and raise up all who have fallen,
let us pray to the Lord:
Lord, have mercy.

Day Fifteen
EVERYONE, ANYONE

READING Revelation 22.12-14, 16-17

'See, I am coming soon; my reward is with me, to repay according to everyone's work. I am the Alpha and the Omega, the first and the last, the beginning and the end.'

Blessed are those who wash their robes, so that they will have the right to the tree of life and may enter the city by the gates.

'It is I, Jesus, who sent my angel to you with this testimony for the churches. I am the root and the descendant of David, the bright morning star.'

> *The Spirit and the bride say, 'Come.'*
> *And let everyone who hears say, 'Come.'*
> *And let everyone who is thirsty come.*
> *Let anyone who wishes take the water of life as a gift.*

REFLECTION

In this last chapter of the last book of the New Testament, we hear Jesus' words to the people in the churches and beyond, spoken through his angel. There is an element of judgement in these words

– repaying everyone according to their work. Nevertheless, we see an invitation that is wide open – the invitation that Jesus the bright morning star is bringing to the world. He is God's gift to the world.

And Jesus has gifts for everyone else. He is the light that gives the right to the tree of life. This right was lost in the Garden of Eden. But this bright star Jesus has worked through his life, death and resurrection to keep the tree of life available and accessible to the world. He keeps the gates open so that people may enter.

This light draws toward him everyone and anyone. This light does not want anyone to perish. It wants to give light to all. As we read in verse 17, 'And let everyone who is thirsty come. Let anyone who wishes take the water of life as a gift.' Come!

MUTHURAJ SWAMY

RESPONSE

How can we extend Jesus' invitation to all people – even those we find it difficult to love?

PRAYER

**Come, Lord Jesus, do not delay;
give courage to your people,
who trust in your love.
By your coming, raise us to share in the joy of your kingdom
on earth as in heaven,
so that we may shine forth as lights for the world.
Amen.**

O Rex Gentium

(22 DECEMBER)

O King of the nations, and their desire,
the corner-stone making both one:
Come and save the human race,
which you fashioned from clay.

cf. Isaiah 28.16; Ephesians 2.14

*O come, Desire of nations! Show
Thy kingly reign on earth below;
Thou Corner-stone, uniting all,
Restore the ruin of our fall.*

*Rejoice! Rejoice! Emmanuel
Shall come to thee, O Israel.*

O King of
the Nations

Day Sixteen
THE PEACE-BRINGER

READING Isaiah 2.2-4

For out of Zion shall go forth instruction,
and the word of the Lord from Jerusalem.
He shall judge between the nations,
and shall arbitrate for many peoples;
they shall beat their swords into ploughshares,
and their spears into pruning-hooks;
nation shall not lift up sword against nation,
neither shall they learn war any more.

REFLECTION

Alfie Bradley's statue shows a tall, fierce, angelic male figure. It is called *Knife Angel* because it is made of 100,000 surrendered knives. Some of the knives sent in for the project still had blood on them. Others had names of loved ones killed by knife crime. All these weapons were blunted and transformed into art.

God gave the prophet Isaiah a vision of something similar. People from all around the world were taking their swords and spears and turning them into farming tools instead. War between nations had ended.

What caused this transformation? Isaiah pictured God ruling from a high mountain in Jerusalem. But the big surprise was that it was not just Jews or the nation of Israel coming to God, the king. Isaiah saw people from *all nations* searching for the king. Many peoples from different countries streamed to that one place. There, the king could teach everyone his ways so all could follow him.

The great news is that God's promised king is not just the Key of David, for Jews only, but King of the Nations, for everyone. Jesus came to bring peace to all nations, including us.

TANYA MARLOW

RESPONSE

Isaiah's vision reminds us that God's invitation of peace is global. Today, which countries might you pray for particularly to know God's peace and wisdom?

PRAYER

In joyful expectation of his coming to our aid, we pray to Jesus:
Come to your world as King of the Nations.

We pray for peace between warring countries,
the laying-down of swords and guns
and for all peoples of the earth to walk in your ways.
Before you rulers will stand in silence.
Maranatha!
Amen. Come, Lord Jesus.

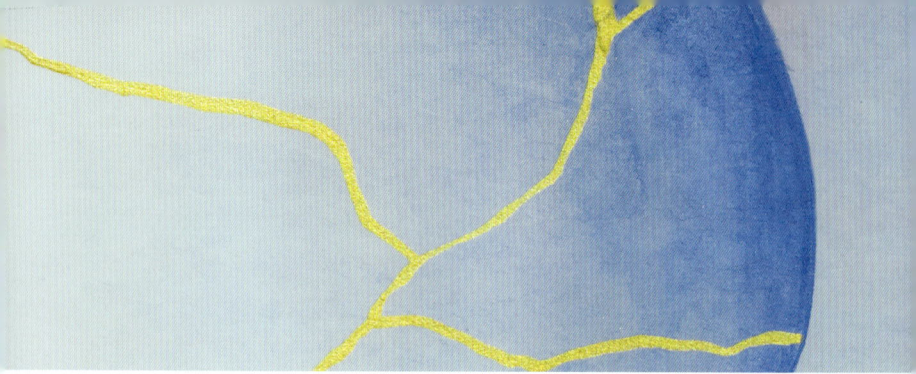

Day Seventeen
THE WALL-BREAKER

READING Ephesians 2.14-22

For he is our peace; in his flesh he has made both groups into one and has broken down the dividing wall, that is, the hostility between us. He has abolished the law with its commandments and ordinances, so that he might create in himself one new humanity in place of the two, thus making peace, and might reconcile both groups to God in one body through the cross, thus putting to death that hostility through it.

REFLECTION

After the Second World War, Germany was split into two nations. People from the East wanted to flee to the rich and free West. To stop this, rulers built the Berlin Wall, which was guarded at gunpoint.

At the time, everyone thought the wall would stand forever, but in 1989, the border was reopened. Strangers from East and West climbed that wall and embraced each other, united at last.

In Paul's day, the big separation was between Jews and everyone else. The 'hostility' between the two groups was like a 'dividing wall'.

But Jesus' death made the two peoples one. Now, non-Jews from every nation could be equal citizens in God's kingdom. That's the first miracle.

The second miracle is even greater. The biggest separation of all is between humanity and God. Sin was the dividing wall we thought would stand forever, but Jesus' death destroyed it.

Picture one dividing wall between heaven and earth, God and humanity, separating top from bottom. Now picture a second wall between people, separating left from right. This is the shape of the cross. In Jesus' outstretched, dying body, all barriers are gone, all are united, all can embrace. Now that's worth celebrating.

TANYA MARLOW

RESPONSE

Jesus brought us peace with God and one another. Which people do we feel hostility towards? Who might God be calling us to embrace this Christmas?

PRAYER

**Most high and holy God,
lift our eyes to your Son
enthroned on Calvary;
and as we behold his meekness,
shatter our earthly pride;
for he is Lord for ever and ever.
Amen.**

Day Eighteen
THE FOUNDATION

READING 1 Peter 2.4-10

Come to him, a living stone, though rejected by mortals yet chosen and precious in God's sight, and like living stones, let yourselves be built into a spiritual house, to be a holy priesthood, to offer spiritual sacrifices acceptable to God through Jesus Christ.

REFLECTION

There are only two groups of people in this world, according to the disciple Peter. One group bases their whole life and identity on Jesus. The other group rejects him.

Peter compares Jesus to a corner-stone, using quotes from the Psalms and the prophet Isaiah. A corner-stone can mean the first stone that everything else is built around. It can also be the finishing stone on an archway that holds everything together. Jesus is like both: the first and last. But if you saw that stone lying around on the ground, you wouldn't realize its importance. That's what refusing Jesus is like.

So, if you are feeling alone, forgotten or rejected this Christmastime, come to Jesus for comfort. Like us, he was rejected, dismissed and even hated. But Jesus was 'chosen and precious in God's sight'. So are you. In Jesus, we are hand-picked by God and never truly alone.

Jesus, Corner-stone of the Church, invites us to build our lives on him. Jesus, King of the Nations, invites everyone to be united as 'God's own people'. This is my prayer: Jesus, keep me returning to you, again and again, my foundation and my saviour.

TANYA MARLOW

RESPONSE

What do you build your life around? Which of Jesus' titles means more to you right now: King of the Nations, or Corner-stone of the Church?

PRAYER

Saving God,
open the gates of righteousness,
that your pilgrim people may enter
and be built into a living temple
on the corner-stone of our salvation,
Jesus Christ our Lord.
Amen.

O Emmanuel

(23 DECEMBER)

O Emmanuel, our King and our lawgiver,
the hope of the nations and their Saviour:
Come and save us, O Lord our God.

cf. Isaiah 7.14

O come, O come, Emmanuel!
Redeem thy captive Israel
That into exile drear is gone,
Far from the face of God's dear Son.

Rejoice! Rejoice! Emmanuel
Shall come to thee, O Israel.

O Emmanuel

Day Nineteen
GOD WITH US

READING Isaiah 7.10-15

'Therefore the Lord himself will give you a sign. Look, the young woman is with child and shall bear a son, and shall name him Immanuel. He shall eat curds and honey by the time he knows how to refuse the evil and choose the good.'

REFLECTION

Fear can make us liars.

Isaiah confronts King Ahaz when the king is terrified at the prospect of war. Isaiah's words both challenge and encourage. The king must stand firm and trust in God. Ahaz, however, is not listening. His faith rests not on God, but on a plan of his own.

Isaiah insists again: he must hear the word of the Lord and seek a sign, the reassurance that God is with him. Ahaz replies with smooth and pious words: he will not put the Lord to the test. This, though, is breathtaking hypocrisy. The truth is that Ahaz does not want the Lord to come anywhere near. He prefers his own version of events.

This hypocrisy triggers a promise and a rebuke from the prophet. The Lord will send a child, a new king, and this child will be the very thing Ahaz cannot face – Immanuel, 'God with us'. More than that, this child will never be a hypocrite – he will always choose the good.

As John's Gospel explains, Christ comes to the world to testify to truth and summon us into truth (John 18.37).

DAVID HOYLE

RESPONSE

In Advent, we look for the God who comes to us. Pause and consider if we are being entirely honest as we sing, 'O Come, Emmanuel'.

PRAYER

God our redeemer,
who prepared the Blessed Virgin Mary
to be the mother of your Son:
grant that, as she looked for his coming as our saviour,
so we may be ready to greet him
when he comes again as our judge.
Amen.

Day Twenty
GOD, OUR ONLY HELP

READING Psalm 80.1-4

Give ear, O Shepherd of Israel,
*   you who lead Joseph like a flock!*
You who are enthroned upon the cherubim, shine forth
*   before Ephraim and Benjamin and Manasseh.*
Stir up your might,
*   and come to save us!*
Restore us, O God;
*   let your face shine, that we may be saved.*

REFLECTION

Beyond the high altar in Westminster Abbey, there is a large golden screen full of all sorts of things that catch the eye. It bears the words: 'The kingdoms of this world are become the kingdoms of our Lord and of his Christ.' It is a slightly loose translation of Revelation 11.15, which speaks of just one 'kingdom'. In the Abbey, where the nations gather and a sovereign is crowned, only one kingdom matters: the Kingdom of God.

David was the famous shepherd king. This psalm, however, cries out to God, for God is the true shepherd of his people. This God is throned in dazzling glory. This God commands tribes and peoples, and this God alone is powerful to save. There is no chance that our best efforts might save us. Left to ourselves, we are lost. Our help is only in the name of our God, whose face shines with a light that exposes our weakness and our need.

'O come, O come, Emmanuel', we sing, 'Come to the nations and save us. Come, for you are our only hope.'

DAVID HOYLE

RESPONSE

Salvation comes to us as sheer gift – not as a reward. How does it feel to receive something you need most as a gift?

PRAYER

We wait for your loving-kindness, O God,
in the midst of your temple.

The glory of the Lord shall be revealed
and all flesh shall see it together.

Show us your mercy, O Lord,
and grant us your salvation.
Amen.

Day Twenty-One
COME TO HELP US

READING Matthew 1.18-23

All this took place to fulfil what had been spoken by the Lord through the prophet:

> *'Look, the virgin shall conceive and bear a son,*
>   *and they shall name him Emmanuel,'*

which means, 'God is with us.'

REFLECTION

Matthew's Gospel begins with a rich, detailed genealogy: 'Jesus the Messiah, the son of David, the son of Abraham … ' Jesus is born into a long family history. Now Matthew rushes on to tell us that this child was foretold by the prophets and heralded by an angel who speaks to Joseph. All history and all hope are summoned up. The drama could not be any greater.

Yet, these great destinies are all contained in a human child – a son for Mary and for Joseph. Joseph, in the midst of anxiety and even shame, is told that in this challenging moment God is suddenly 'with us'. It is shocking. It is barely credible.

The twentieth-century Dominican philosopher Herbert McCabe famously preached about the beginning of this Gospel. He noted just how human the story is: 'Jesus did not belong to the nice clean world ... He belonged to a family of murderers, cheats and cowards.'

This is what we mean when we speak of Emmanuel, 'God with us': 'He belonged to us, and came to help us – no wonder he came to a bad end and gave us some hope.'

DAVID HOYLE

RESPONSE

Pause in wonder, remembering that God comes to us in the one form we can recognize – as one of us.

PRAYER

Welcome, all wonders in one sight!
Eternity shut in a span;
Summer in winter; day in night;
Heaven in earth, and God in man.
Great little one, whose all-embracing birth
Lifts earth to heaven, stoops heav'n to earth!

Magnificat
(The Song of Mary)

✝

'My soul magnifies the Lord,
and my spirit rejoices in God my Saviour,
for he has looked with favour on the lowliness of his servant.
Surely, from now on all generations will call me blessed;
for the Mighty One has done great things for me,
and holy is his name.
His mercy is for those who fear him
from generation to generation.
He has shown strength with his arm;
he has scattered the proud in the thoughts of their hearts.
He has brought down the powerful from their thrones,
and lifted up the lowly;
he has filled the hungry with good things,
and sent the rich away empty.
He has helped his servant Israel,
in remembrance of his mercy,
according to the promise he made to our ancestors,
to Abraham and to his descendants for ever.'

Luke 1.46–55

Glory to the Father and to the Son
and to the Holy Spirit;
as it was in the beginning is now
and shall be for ever. Amen.

Magnificat

Day Twenty-Two
PRAISE! MAGNIFY!

READING Luke 1.46-49

And Mary said,

'My soul magnifies the Lord,
and my spirit rejoices in God my Saviour,
for he has looked with favour on the lowliness of his servant.
Surely, from now on all generations will call me blessed;
for the Mighty One has done great things for me,
and holy is his name.'

REFLECTION

All the antiphons we've been thinking about this Advent belong to the central text we now consider. Mary's song as recorded in Luke's Gospel, known by its first word in Latin: Magnificat. *Praise! Magnify!*

The genre of this song is what we call 'doxology' – that is, it's an outpouring of praise and joy directed towards God. God is the focus and subject of this song, even if, in English, the first word is 'My'.

This balance perhaps sums up the whole meaning of the canticle. It is an intimate connection between the human and divine, a song sung in time towards eternity.

Mary was a young Jewish woman in a particular time and place. Yet she bears into the world the eternal presence and nature of God. Her time is now, yes. But she looks forward into the future as she tells the generations to come – she tells *us* – 'This is for you too.'

Mary stands at the crossroads between time and eternity. She is an echo of the woman in the Book of Proverbs (chapter 8) who stands 'at the crossroads' and calls for justice. In doing so, Mary embraces her vocation, soul-piercing as it will turn out to be.

LUCY WINKETT

RESPONSE

How does it feel to be connected, through Mary's song, to the past two thousand years? And the two thousand years to come?

PRAYER

Eternal Word of God,
we thank you that you came to us in the midst of time
and pray that you may be born in us
as we join in the song of Mary.
Amen.

Day Twenty-Three
RADICAL

READING Luke 1.50-53

'His mercy is for those who fear him
from generation to generation.
He has shown strength with his arm;
he has scattered the proud in the thoughts of their hearts.
He has brought down the powerful from their thrones,
and lifted up the lowly;
he has filled the hungry with good things,
and sent the rich away empty.'

REFLECTION

Jesus' ministry began in a synagogue in Nazareth when he read from the book of Isaiah. Isaiah's prophecy speaks of the Messiah bringing good news to the poor. But before this, the good news was also proclaimed by Mary.

The verses from today's reading are genuinely radical. They are so radical that the Magnificat was sometimes banned by regimes around the world, afraid of its power. This is a vision, like Isaiah's, of a world made new, a world turned upside down (or more accurately the right way up).

Mary's challenge to 'the proud' is a provocative and enduring reflection on the human condition. She meditates on the power of God, who scatters 'the proud in the thoughts of their hearts'. It's not just about material wealth and power. Mary praises God for lifting up those who are not confident in their virtue but know their need for grace and mercy. The echo of Mary's song can be heard in Jesus' teaching: 'Blessed are the poor in spirit'.

We often emphasize Jesus' nature as the son of God. But in Mary's radical vision of this new and just society, we can see he is his mother's son too.

LUCY WINKETT

RESPONSE

Where do you see people suffering injustice? How can you join in Mary's proclaiming of justice and peace this Christmas?

PRAYER

O God of mercy, help us to be humble in our thoughts.
Let not the needy be forgotten;
nor the hope of the poor be taken away.
Guide the meek in judgement;
and teach your ways to the gentle.
Lord, remember your people;
whom you have redeemed.
Amen.

Day Twenty-Four
VISION

READING Luke 1.54-55

'He has helped his servant Israel,
in remembrance of his mercy,
according to the promise he made to our ancestors,
to Abraham and to his descendants for ever.'

REFLECTION

The Magnificat is said or sung every day in cathedrals, churches and communities around the world. But during Advent, the antiphons that surround it give it a special resonance.

The Magnificat is the enduring melody that resounds as God emerges into the world. The antiphons give us images of Christ as key, as root, as the morning star. These images help us to see Mary's story in a bigger, eternal context.

A mysterious angelic messenger tells her that she is the *Theotokos*, the bearer of God into the world. In this season, Mary's song stands out as the central axis of the doctrine of the incarnation. God will come into the world through her. Christ will come in the vulnerability of a baby and with the light and power of the sun.

The Magnificat is less a lullaby than a call to (peaceful) arms. It is a vision of God's world as God would have it. Accompanied by the 'O' antiphons, it takes its place not only as a societal blueprint but as a vision of the universe as it is meant to be.

Singing the Magnificat in Advent puts a Christ-centred view into the life of the Church. All humanity is invited to sing the song of Mary, the mother of God: inspiring, provocative and awesome.

LUCY WINKETT

RESPONSE

Pause and think back on the different images we read about this Advent. How do they reveal to you the saving work of God in the world?

PRAYER

Almighty God,
give us grace to cast away the works of darkness
and to put on the armour of light,
now in the time of this mortal life,
in which your Son Jesus Christ came to us in great humility;
that on the last day,
when he shall come again in his glorious majesty
to judge the living and the dead,
we may rise to the life immortal.
Amen.

Church House Publishing
Church House
27 Great Smith Street
London SW1P 3AZ

www.chpublishing.co.uk

ISBN   978 1 78140 519 2 (Paperback)
         978 1 78140 520 8 (e-ISBN)

Published 2025 by Church House Publishing

The opinions expressed in this book are those of the contributors and do not necessarily reflect the official policy of the General Synod or The Archbishops' Council of the Church of England.

EU GPSR Authorised Representative
LOGOS EUROPE, 9 rue Nicolas Poussin, 17000, LA ROCHELLE, France
E-mail: Contact@logoseurope.eu

No part of this book may be used or reproduced in any manner for the purpose of training artificial intelligence technologies or systems.

Cover artwork: SunYoung Kim
Cover and internal design: www.penguinboy.net
Editing and typesetting by Hugh Hillyard-Parker, Edinburgh
Printed and bound in England by CPI Group (UK) Ltd